PYTHAGORAS

MATHEMATICIAN AND MYSTIC

THE
GREATEST
GREEK PHILOSOPHERS

PYTHAGORAS

MATHEMATICIAN AND MYSTIC

LOUIS C. COAKLEY & DIMITRA KARAMANIDES

ROSEN
PUBLISHING
NEW YORK

To my mom and dad—DK

Published in 2016 by The Rosen Publishing Group, Inc.
29 East 21st Street, New York, NY 10010

First Edition

Library of Congress Cataloging-in-Publication Data

Coakley, Louis C., author.
Pythagoras: mathematician and mystic/Louis C. Coakley and Dimitra Karamanides. —First edition.
     pages cm.—(The greatest Greek philosophers)
Includes bibliographical references and index.
ISBN 978-1-4994-6132-9 (library bound)
1. Pythagoras—Juvenile literature. 2. Philosophers—Greece—Biography—Juvenile literature. 3. Mathematicians—Greece—Biography—Juvenile literature. I. Karamanides, Dimitra, author. II. Title.
B243.C63 2015
182.2—dc23
[B]
                                                                    2014048889

Manufactured in the United States of America

CONTENTS

If the name Pythagoras sounds familiar, that's most likely thanks to the Pythagorean theorem. The Pythagorean theorem is probably the best-known theorem in all of math. A theorem is a statement that can be proven based on other statements that have already been proven. Theorems are an important part of the study of geometry. The Pythagorean theorem, which is often written with the equation $a^2 + b^2 = c^2$, states that

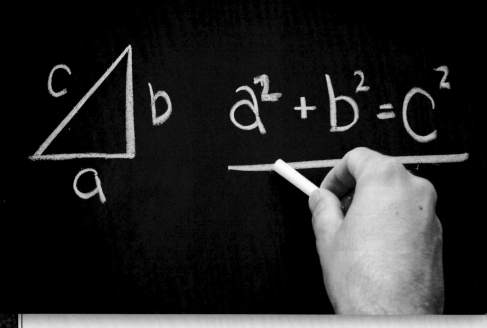

The Pythagorean theorem makes it possible to find the length of any side of a right triangle as long as you know the lengths of the other two sides.

if you add together the squares of the two shorter sides of a right triangle, they will equal the square of the longer side.

Pythagoras, after whom the theorem is named, lived in ancient Greece. During his lifetime, Pythagoras's pursuit of knowledge ranged across subjects as different as the gods, astronomy, numbers, diet, and music. Pythagoras was more than a mathematician; he was also a philosopher, musician, and religious leader. While modern

Since there aren't any images of Pythagoras from his own time, we're not sure what he really looked like. This engraving of him was published in 1584 in France.

people tend to see these as contradictory roles, to Pythagoras they were all connected.

7

Historians estimate that Pythagoras lived between 569 and 495 BCE, but the exact dates of his life are unknown. In fact, there is much about Pythagoras that is unknown. Most of the evidence scholars have for the details of his life is based on the accounts of writers who lived seven hundred to eight hundred years after his death. In the absence of any primary sources, this volume relies on these traditional accounts. However, it should be pointed out that some of this biographical information is thought to be inaccurate or legendary by modern scholars.

Scholars also have their doubts about which of the discoveries and insights attributed to Pythagoras were actually his work. Much may have been the work of the Pythagoreans, as Pythagoras's followers in his own time and in the centuries after his death were known. Whether he was the source or just the inspiration, though, Pythagoras had a real impact on the ancient Greek world, one that is still felt today.

CHAPTER ONE

GROWING UP IN IONIA

The traditional date given for Pythagoras's birth is 569 BCE. He was born on Samos, an island that was part of Ionia, a portion of the ancient Greek world that was made up of Greek-speaking settlements along the west coast of what is now Turkey but was then known as Asia Minor. While Ionia is sometimes more broadly defined, the core of it consisted of Samos, the island of Chios, and the mainland cities of Miletus, Myus, Priene, Ephesus, Colophon, Lebedus, Teos, Clazomanae, Erythrae, and Phocaea.

Samos is a small island, only about 184 square miles (476 square kilometers) large. Despite this apparent disadvantage, it played an important role in ancient Greek politics and culture. The island's distance from mainland Greece wasn't a disadvantage either. The Greeks

Ancient Greece included communities on both sides of the Aegean Sea, as you can see on this map of Greece at the time of the Peloponnesian War (431–404 BCE).

were a seafaring people and Samos lies in the Aegean, the sea that was central to the history and culture of Greece.

Pythagoras's mother, who was known as Parthenis, is believed to have come from one of Samos's most aristocratic families. Pythagoras's father, Mnesarchus, was a wealthy merchant of Phoenician descent who had settled on Samos.

THE PHOENICIANS

The Phoenicians established several independent, powerful cities on the east coast of the Mediterranean, the most powerful of which were Tyre, Sidon, Byblos, and Arwad. The territory that Phoenicia occupied is now part of Lebanon and Syria. In part because their opportunities for agriculture were limited, the Phoenicians became a civilization of seagoing merchants. Phoenicia's primary resources were cedar trees (the famous "cedars of Lebanon") and murex shells, which were used to make a purple dye that was prized throughout the ancient world. The civilization's craftsmen were well regarded and produced textiles, as well as objects made out of wood and metal.

Known for their skill as sailors, the Phoenicians traveled throughout the Mediterranean and beyond (for example, they are known to have sailed to Britain to obtain tin). The Phoenicians established colonies in North Africa, Spain, Sicily, Sardinia, and the Balearic Islands. Among these was Carthage, in what is now Tunisia, which became a powerful empire in its own right.

Mnesarchus was granted Samian citizenship because he provided food for the Samians during a famine. Mnesarchus's business was trade, and he made frequent trips to all the ports around the Mediterranean Sea. As a child, Pythagoras often accompanied his father on these trips. They traveled as far as southern Italy, the place where Pythagoras would eventually establish his famous school.

Mnesarchus provided his son with every opportunity for excellence. As a child, Pythagoras began what would turn out to be a long and comprehensive education. Mnesarchus provided Pythagoras with tutors who taught subjects as varied as philosophy, athletics, music, and painting.

PHERECYDES

The first of Pythagoras's notable tutors was Pherecydes of Syros. When Pythagoras was young, his father sent him to the Greek island of Syros to study with Pherecydes, who had been initiated into the Temple of Apollo on Delos. Delos was a tiny island in the Aegean Sea that was sacred to Greeks because many believed that the island was the birthplace of Apollo and his sister, the goddess Artemis. People from all parts of the Greek world made pilgrimages to Delos to honor Apollo.

Pherecydes was clearly a strong influence on his young student. Many key points of Pherecydes's philosophy appear later as fundamentals in Pythagoras's own teachings. Pherecydes emphasized the study of music, a subject that would interest Pythagoras for his entire life,

This bust of Pherecydes on the island of Syros honors the philosopher who called the island home more than 2,500 years ago.

becoming one of the cornerstones of Pythagorean philosophy. Also, Pherecydes was one of the first Greeks who taught about the immortality of the soul, specifically that the soul moves from one body to another from one lifetime to the next. Pythagoras preached this concept of the "transmigration of the soul," known today as reincarnation, as a basic tenet of his beliefs.

Perhaps the strongest influence that Pherecydes had on Pythagoras was in his powerful respect for the gods, whom Pherecydes believed deserved study and reverence. In his search for a complete understanding of the natural world, Pherecydes even went so far as to invent new gods who would help explain the workings of nature and the universe. Pythagoras had a similar mission. Though remembered primarily as a mathematician, it is important to note that all of Pythagoras's theories, even those concerning numbers, were philosophical attempts to bring all things, including humans, into harmony with the gods.

MILETUS

Although Pythagoras traveled widely as a young man, he spent the majority of his youth at Samos. Eventually, however, he decided that it was time to pursue an education abroad. He was still quite a young man when he set off for Miletus to study with some of Greece's most famous philosophers.

The city of Miletus, a thriving port, was also part of Ionia. During the second half of the sixth century BCE, it was home to Greece's first clearly defined philosophical movement, the Ionian school. It is sometimes also called the Milesian school, after the city around which it grew. The philosophers mainly associated with this school were Thales, Anaximander, and Anaximenes. Thales headed the school and served as Anaximander's tutor. During his stay in Miletus, Pythagoras studied with both of these highly respected men.

Miletus continued to be one of the most important cities in the ancient Greek world through the third century CE. These Milesian ruins date from around 50 CE.

The most distinctive characteristic of the Milesian philosophical movement was its attempt to explain the world by material means. In other words, its members believed that knowledge of the universe was gained through experience and observation. They stated that humans begin to understand the world by testing theories, which are carefully plotted and provable. Known as the empirical method today, this is exactly how scientists learn about the world. During the sixth century BCE, however, empiricism was a revolutionary idea.

Before the Ionian school of thought gained influence, thinkers explained all natural phenomena—such as rain, wind, sunrise, and sunset—as resulting from the actions of the gods. The behavior of the gods was mysterious, and therefore, there was no point in people trying to understand the way that the world worked. Thales and his fellow philosophers disagreed. These Ionian philosophers studied subjects ranging from mathematics and engineering to geography and agriculture, to name just a few. They also pursued cosmology—the study of the origin, current state, and future of the universe—and astronomy, which is the study of the movement of bodies in outer space. According to the Ionian philosophers, all things in the universe were part of a whole. To understand the way things worked, one first needed to find out what the world was made of. Their interest in empiricism may make it seem as if they rejected the existence of gods altogether, but the Ionians' philosophy claimed that the gods were always present in all things. This made it even more valuable to observe nature closely, so that they could both learn about the natural world through study and witness physical manifestations or signs of the divine all around them. Since they tried to understand how all things in nature worked, these Ionian thinkers became known as the natural philosophers (or *physici* in Greek), meaning "those who study things in nature." They were the first people in Western thought whom we might describe as scientists in a modern sense.

THALES AND ANAXIMANDER

For a student as curious as Pythagoras, a stop in Miletus to study with these philosophers must have been irresistible. Soon after his arrival in Miletus, Pythagoras became a student of Thales's. He was the Ionian school's founding father. Not only was Thales the founder and leader of the Ionian school, he was also respected throughout the Greek world. More than one hundred years later, the philosopher Plato would list Thales as one of the Seven Sages, a list composed of men whom Plato considered wise beyond all others.

Thales's accomplishments were astonishing for the sixth century BCE. He correctly predicted a solar eclipse and was the author of five mathematical theorems. He even used geometry to determine the size of the sun and moon. It is not difficult to see why such an impressive thinker would become a major influence on Pythagoras.

While in Miletus, Pythagoras also became a student of the philosopher Anaximander, who had once studied under Thales. Anaximander's contributions to philosophy included

This bust of Thales is in the Capitoline Museum, in Rome. The philosopher Aristotle called Thales the founder of natural philosophy, the study of the natural world that evolved into science.

the concept of a universe that is infinite, or unlimited. He was the first person to say that Earth was a free-floating body in space and to draw a map of the world. Anaximander also was responsible for teaching Pythagoras to avoid meat and wine.

This Roman mosaic shows Anaximander holding a sundial. Anaximander is traditionally credited with introducing the sundial to the Greek world.

Thales's and Anaximander's influence on Pythagoras was undeniable throughout his life and work. From complex concepts related to cosmology and mathematics to ideas as simple as avoiding wine, the Ionian philosophers' teachings left their mark on Pythagoras. It is no surprise that when Thales recommended that Pythagoras continue his studies in Egypt, Pythagoras listened.

Instead of boarding a ship and heading straight for Egypt, however, Pythagoras traveled slowly down the eastern Mediterranean Sea. Along the way, he made stops in Phoenicia and other lands, familiarizing himself with a variety of thinkers and religious leaders. Pythagoras learned something new wherever he went and added these new ideas to his own developing philosophy.

CHAPTER TWO

TRAVELS FAR AND WIDE

During Pythagoras's lifetime, a new scientific age was dawning in Greece. In Egypt, Babylon, and other nations east of Greece, however, similar advances in mathematics, physics, astronomy, and geometry had been made centuries earlier. The Greeks considered Egypt to be the birthplace of mathematics. In addition, the Babylonians used what we now call the Pythagorean theorem more than one thousand years before Pythagoras.

Both Egyptian and Babylonian priests had long observed the night skies and attempted to explain the movement of the planets and stars. In these countries, people used geometry extensively for construction and agricultural purposes. While Greek mathematics was only in its infancy, these nations had been fine-tuning their mathematical and astronomical theories for centuries. For

Priests played an important role in ancient Egyptian culture. This painting of a priest making an offering comes from the tomb of Ramesses IX.

curious students such as Pythagoras, this "new" knowledge was there just waiting to be absorbed.

STUDYING IN EGYPT

Although Pythagoras came to Egypt during the sixth century BCE, Egypt's powerful tradition in mathematics had reached its peak more than one thousand years earlier. The Egyptians' expertise was in applying mathematics to very practical uses. No other people up to that point had applied mathematics as constructively as the Egyptians had. They used it to create the pyramids, to ease trade with detailed accounting systems, and to measure land. *Geometry* is from the Greek word meaning "the measuring of land." This practice started on the banks of the Nile River, which flooded every year. When the water receded after the annual flood, contours in the land changed and had to be measured again. It is no surprise, then, that the Egyptians were masters of "land counting," or geometry.

Other than the study of geometry, we do not have many specifics about what mathematics Pythagoras learned during the years that he spent in Egypt. However, we know that Pythagoras did a great deal more than study mathematics. He was the first Greek to delve into Egyptian religion, an undertaking that had a profound effect on his philosophies later in life. Perhaps he studied Egyptian religion because the religious centers in Egypt were also the centers for learning. Priests were Egypt's principal scholars. A chance to enter into the Egyptian priesthood must have been an opportunity he relished.

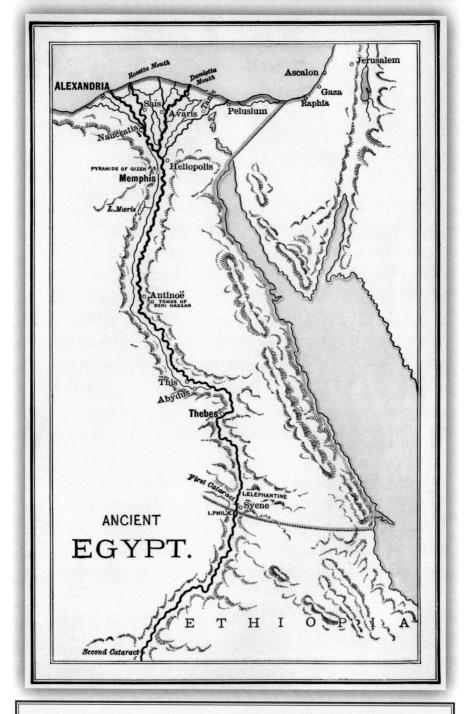

You can see the religious centers of Memphis, Thebes, and Heliopolis on this map. Hermopolis is not shown but was roughly across the Nile River from Antinoë.

It was not easy for a Greek to be accepted into the long and intensive training of an Egyptian priest. In the end, Pythagoras's seriousness and persistence must have won over Egypt's religious leaders, for Pythagoras did indeed train with Egyptian priests. Before leaving Egypt, Pythagoras was initiated into all four of the country's major religious centers: Memphis, Thebes, Heliopolis, and Hermopolis.

EGYPTIAN RELIGION

The religious beliefs of the ancient Egyptians were not uniform but varied over time and in different parts of the country. Different stories of how life came into being were associated with each of the major Egyptian religious centers. Heliopolis's priests named Atum, also known as Atum-Re, as the first of the gods. He was worshiped there alongside eight gods descended from him, collectively known as the Ennead of Heliopolis. In Hermopolis, a group of eight gods, known as the Ogdoad, were honored. The priests in Thebes taught that their city was the site of the first land and the creation of the gods, starting with Amun. At Memphis, priests held that the god Ptah was the creator. Ptah was the god of craftsmen and thought; his creation of the world was a mental one.

Pythagoras was exposed to a variety of Egyptian ideas during the years he spent in these four Egyptian centers of learning. As a student, he learned about the Egyptian concept of the human soul. According to the Egyptians, the soul evolves and lives on after the death of the body. This idea appeared later in Pythagoras's teachings. He also studied Egyptian astronomy. Crystal-clear Egyptian night skies made this country ideal for stargazing. Egyptian priests were astronomers as well as holy men. While studying with the priests, Pythagoras formed views about the heavens, which later played a central role in Pythagorean thought.

In 525 BCE, the Persians, led by King Cambyses, attacked and overran Egypt. As a result, many Egyptian priests were exiled to Babylon, which the Persians had also captured. Pythagoras was one of the priests exiled there. Babylon lay between the Tigris and Euphrates rivers, in what is now Iraq.

STUDYING IN BABYLON

The details of Pythagoras's life in Babylon are rather fuzzy. Historians believe that Pythagoras studied with the city's priests, known as magi, during his exile

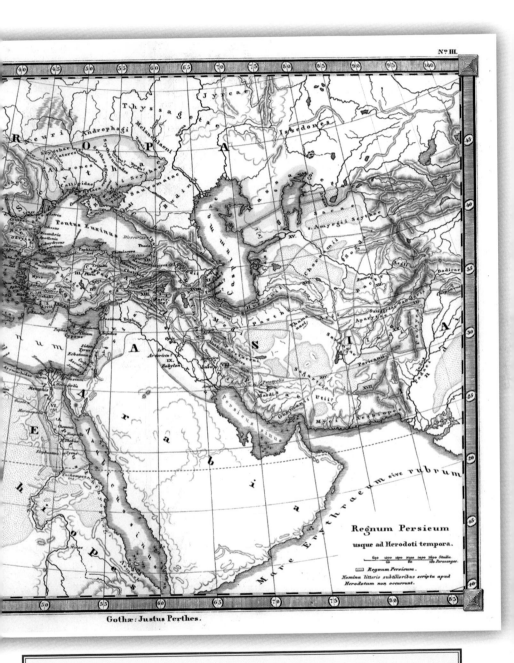

Several dynasties are known as the Persian Empire. This map shows the one that drove Pythagoras from Egypt, also called the Achaemenid Empire, in the early sixth century BCE.

there. Just as in Egypt, Babylonian religious centers were also the main centers of learning. Pythagoras's studies with the magi would have focused on subjects ranging from religion and mathematics to music and astrology.

Ancient Babylonians were noted for their expertise in the field of astronomy. They were the first people to use arithmetic to predict planetary movement. They were also among the first to try to create an accurate calendar based on the movement of the planets and stars. The magi preserved many of their observations on cuneiform tablets. Cuneiform was an ancient method of writing that involved drawing abstract pictures with reeds on clay tablets.

Although the Babylonians were very successful at charting the movement of heavenly bodies, they were not interested in astronomy for purely scientific

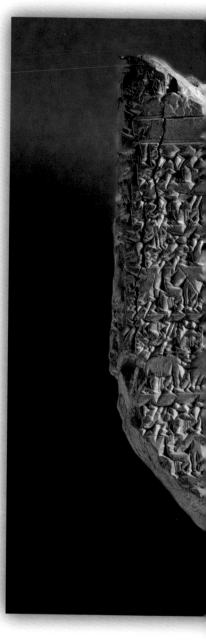

purposes. They had a mystical belief that the movement of the planets and stars held the keys to understanding

This astronomical tablet from the city of Kish, in what is now Iraq, records the risings and settings of the planet Venus over a six-year period. It dates from the seventh century BCE.

and predicting events on Earth, a concept very similar to what we call astrology today. The Babylonians used their recorded observations to make predictions about the forces of nature, human behavior, and future events. Even kings consulted with astrologers before making important decisions.

As a student of philosophy and mathematics, exile in Babylon was actually a lucky turn of events for Pythagoras. Like Egypt, Babylon boasted an old and expert tradition in mathematics. Babylonian mathematics was based on the number sixty, a number system borrowed from the Sumerians. Today we use ten as the base of our numbering system. Historians believe that the Babylonians had been using the so-called Pythagorean theorem more than one thousand years before Pythagoras came to the city.

The influence that Pythagoras's years in Egypt and Babylon had on him cannot be overestimated. The legendary scholars of these nations gave Pythagoras enough knowledge to fill several lifetimes. In subjects ranging from mathematics to religion, both countries' scholars provided Pythagoras with an education he could not have hoped to receive in Greece at that time. Pythagoras's many years in the east had finally prepared him to make the transition from student to teacher.

RETURNING TO SAMOS

After leaving Babylon, Pythagoras planned to open a school on the island of Samos, his childhood home. Instead of going straight to Samos, however, he traveled widely throughout Greece. Perhaps he did this to catch up on all the latest developments in Greek philosophy and knowledge that he had missed during his years in the East.

Once Pythagoras returned to Samos, he wasted no time in setting up his school, which became known as the Semicircle. Centuries after Pythagoras's death, the people of Samos still held important meetings at the site of this famous school. Pythagoras's school on Samos focused on two main subjects, philosophy and mathematics. Unfortunately, because the school was short-lived and secretive, historians do not know many details about what Pythagoras taught during these years.

By this point in time, Pythagoras had become famous throughout Greece. Philosophers from all parts of Greece came to visit him on his home island. Given his fame and wealthy background, many expected that Pythagoras would live comfortably in Samos. Instead, he sometimes taught and possibly lived alone in a small cave where he spent much of his time contemplating mathematics. After all the years abroad, Pythagoras had not changed much from the curious young man who had set off for Miletus. Like the serious boy who abstained from wine and meat, the famous philosopher still lived simply, avoiding material comforts.

PROBLEMS IN SAMOS

It became clear to Pythagoras that Samos might not be the ideal place for him to establish a school. Although he

had become famous, he had some difficulty attracting the type of student that he wanted in the Semicircle. One of the reasons may be that the Greeks of Samos did not accept his teaching methods. Historians describe Pythagoras's teaching method as symbolic and typical of Egyptian teaching methods. For example, numbers did not only represent values for Pythagoras. They also had spiritual meaning. So a question or problem posed by Pythagoras that on its surface seemed mathematical, might in fact have been a question concerning the gods or other spiritual matters. Greeks were used to a more straightforward approach to teaching. Also, the Greeks may simply not have been prepared for the type of mathematics Pythagoras was trying to introduce. Whatever the reasons, there was much resistance to Pythagoras's teachings and his students.

Other accounts say that what convinced Pythagoras to leave Samos was his inability to focus exclusively on his teaching. The people of Samos held a great respect for Pythagoras and turned to him for political advice on a regular basis. This was a major drain on his time—time that he wished to devote to studying and teaching. Even worse, as Samos's most famous philosopher, Pythagoras was expected to meet with every important public

In Pythagoras's time, Samos was the site of an important temple to the goddess Hera. This column is part of the ruins of the temple, which was rebuilt several times.

official who visited the island. Pythagoras wanted to serve his native land, but he did not want to sacrifice his pursuit of knowledge to do so.

At any rate, it became clear to Pythagoras that Samos was not the place to build the school of his dreams. Pythagoras decided he would have to leave his native land in order to establish a great philosophical school. Having made up his mind to leave Samos again, Pythagoras wasted no time. He set sail for Croton, a Greek colony hundreds of miles away from his native island. Pythagoras may have visited Croton as a child during one of his father's business trips. There, the most important chapter of his life would begin.

CHAPTER THREE

SETTLING IN CROTON

The people of Croton were honored by Pythagoras's decision to call their city home. According to tradition, when Pythagoras arrived by ship in Croton around 518 BCE, the harbor's shore was crowded with people eagerly waiting to see and hear the wise man speak. He did not disappoint them. From the moment Pythagoras set foot on Croton, the colony was never the same. Pythagoras and his new followers, many of whom were local leaders, influenced everything from Croton's politics and economy to its family life. They did this by establishing a school that became much more than a center of learning; for many, it provided an entire way of life.

As early as the eighth century BCE, the Greeks had started to establish colonies in southern Italy and Sicily. By the fifth century

This eighteenth-century map shows southern Italy, Corsica, and Sardinia in ancient times, including the settlements that made up Magna Graecia.

BCE, southern Italy was home to many powerful Greek colonies. Southern Italy was known as Magna Graecia, meaning "greater Greece." Croton was one of the colonies on Magna Graecia.

Croton (modern-day Crotone, Italy) was established almost two hundred years before Pythagoras's arrival. During Pythagoras's time, Croton was at the peak of its power, famed for its medicine and Olympic athletes. Its main source of income was agriculture. Although Croton was far from the distractions of Samos, it was still part of the Greek world. Croton's combination of physical remoteness and intellectual connection to Greece made it the ideal location for Pythagoras's new school.

PYTHAGORAS'S SCHOOL

The school that Pythagoras established on Croton would become his principal legacy and the vehicle by which his philosophical and mathematical theories would spread in the future. At its height, its students numbered approximately 2,500. The school was shrouded in secrecy during Pythagoras's time because he believed that knowledge was dangerous in the hands of the uninitiated. Yet historians have been able to learn about some of its practices and teachings. Not until almost one hundred years after Pythagoras's death did a few followers finally drop the veil of silence that covered Pythagorean learning by revealing the school's complex inner workings.

The emphasis Pythagoras placed on secrecy led the society to adopt very complex and indirect teaching methods. Lessons were anything but straightforward. All knowledge was encoded in stories and sayings that often had little to do with the actual information being taught. The purpose of teaching through the use of parables, sayings, and codes was to keep information out of the hands of the uninitiated. Egypt's influence on Pythagoras was again apparent. Egyptian priests had been transmitting information symbolically for centuries, in the hope of keeping it hidden from ordinary people.

The Pythagorean society was not a school open only to young men, as was typical at the time. It admitted people of any age and gender, many of whom lived in the school full-time. These full-time, core students, who numbered about five hundred, were known as *mathematikoi*. The students were not permitted to marry and could not own anything privately. When their initiation into the school began, they had to turn all private possessions over to the society. The students lived communally with the other mathematikoi and were no longer allowed to eat

MIRACULOUS STORIES

Many ancient sources tell us that Pythagoras was both divine and capable of performing miracles. Indeed, some of his followers believed him to be the son of the god Apollo. Some authors claimed that Pythagoras had a thigh made of solid gold and that he could communicate with animals. According to tradition, Pythagoras confronted a wild bear that had been damaging property and threatening people. After Pythagoras reasoned with the animal, it quietly walked away and never bothered anybody again. Another skill Pythagoras was said to have had was the ability to be in two places at the same time. His followers believed that he taught students in Metapontum, Italy, and Tauromenium, Sicily, two localities separated by about 200 miles (322 km), on the same day. Some believed, too, that Pythagoras was capable of predicting earthquakes and calming rough winds.

meat. The mathematikoi were more than students—they were also Pythagoras's devoted disciples.

The other two thousand students who made up the rest of the society were known as *akousmatikoi*, which means "listeners" in Greek. These students were given this name because, unlike the mathematikoi, they were not permitted to see Pythagoras, who gave his lectures to them from behind a veil. They were permitted to live with their families in their own homes and retain their private property. They were also allowed to eat meat. The akousmatikoi paid a price for living under a looser set of rules. Unlike the mathematikoi, the akousmatikoi were not permitted to learn Pythagoras's most sacred teachings, including high-level mathematics.

VERY HIGH STANDARDS

Pythagoras had many willing students on Croton, but he did not believe that every person was qualified to be given the knowledge that he possessed. Only a select few had the qualifications that Pythagoras was looking for in mathematikoi. According to Pythagoras, gaining knowledge was an attempt on the part of men and women to come closer to the gods. He believed that the soul developed from one lifetime to the next until it reached a divine level. In order to reach this level, one had to be prepared to devote one's life completely to the pursuit of knowledge. Pythagoras was not just looking for students; he was looking to find disciples. To that end, Pythagoras created a rigorous qualification process that all potential mathematikoi had to endure.

Before a student began his or her training in the Pythagorean society, he or she had to pass a personality test of sorts conducted by Pythagoras himself. In order to assess the student's likelihood of success, Pythagoras looked at

This painting by the nineteenth-century Russian artist Fyodor Andreyevich Bronnikov shows Pythagoras and his followers greeting the dawn with music.

how the student spoke and laughed and how the student spent his or her free time. He also studied what made the student happy or sad. The potential student's relationships to family and friends were also carefully noted. Even body language was studied and analyzed during the selection process. Finally, Pythagoras tested potential students for memory and the ability to learn.

If a student was lucky enough to make it through this screening process, he or she would then be required to give up all personal possessions and enter the school on a full-time basis. The novice student was required to take a five-year vow of silence. Pythagoras considered silence essential to learning. Perhaps his many years as a student in Egypt had taught him that. Pythagoras believed that if a person was able to endure five years of complete silence, he or she clearly demonstrated a willingness and ability to learn. And learning, after all, was the sole focus of this society.

Once a Pythagorean disciple passed all of the master's tests and was admitted into the community on a full-time basis, he or she concentrated on one area of study, depending on his or her interests and abilities. Subjects ranged from music and medicine to mathematics. The students were expected to excel in their chosen field, and many did. Some historians claim that some of the theories attributed to Pythagoras were, in fact, the work of his gifted students.

A student was required to learn well and quickly, but not all students were able to meet Pythagoras's high standards. The consequences were harsh for students who failed. In addition to being expelled immediately from the school, Pythagoras and the other students would shun the failed student for the rest of his or her life. The Pythagorean society would set up a monument to the failed student, as if he or she had passed away and no longer existed. When other students met the expelled student on the street, they pretended that he or she was not there. It was perhaps little consolation to those who failed that they received twice the value of whatever money or possessions they had brought with them into the society.

PURE LIVES

Pythagoras's school offered a great deal more to its students than just the study of mathematics and philosophy. For the initiated, it provided an all-encompassing guide for living, governing every daily action, from diet and sleep schedules to worship and social interaction among students. Pythagoras believed that the way one lived played a crucial role in one's ability to learn. A Pythagorean disciple had to live a pure life in order to follow the path toward a divine soul. The quest for a pure life started by following the rules that Pythagoras considered essential for all of his disciples. These included communal possessions, harmony between friends and family members, worship of the gods, honoring of the dead, fair and good government, a dedicated pursuit of knowledge, silence, and moderation in all things.

The Pythagoreans did not live poorly, but they did live simply. In the words of Iamblichus, a third century-CE neo-Pythagorean, "A temple, indeed, should be adorned with gifts, but the soul with disciplines." Pythagoreans shared all physical possessions, including money, property, and clothing. Comfort was the ideal, but luxury was considered sinful. Moderation in all things was the goal for which they strived. Students were urged to listen carefully and to speak only when necessary. Even emotions that were too extreme were frowned upon. A student was encouraged to keep his or her desires and appetites in check.

According to the Pythagoreans, a healthy body made for a healthy mind. As a result, the society in Croton had strict rules governing its students' diet. For reasons that are not clear to us today, all Pythagoreans were banned from eating beans of any sort. Some historians believe that this was a practice that Pythagoras adopted during his years in Egypt. Also, the mathematikoi were barred completely from eating meat, while the akousmatikoi were permitted only small quantities. Even the akousmatikoi, however, were not allowed to eat the brain or heart of an animal. The restrictions on meat eating make sense in light of the fact that Pythagoras believed that souls migrate from one creature to another. According to Pythagoras, the soul of a dead friend might be living in the body of the animal you intend to eat.

The Pythagorean prohibition on wine was notable because wine was central to ancient Greek culture. This vase painting of a man drinking wine dates from around 520–510 BCE.

The society also restricted wine, a staple of the ancient Greek diet. According to some historians, the mathematikoi were not permitted any wine except that which was necessary for worshipping the gods. Akousmatikoi, since they were the more casual students, were allowed to drink wine in moderation. Drunkenness of any sort was completely unacceptable. The Pythagoreans specifically discouraged pregnant women from drinking alcohol, just as doctors do today. For his initiates, Pythagoras also prescribed specific ways to interact with friends and family. The basic rule was kindness and respect between all parties. Friends were encouraged to treat each other respectfully. Pythagoras himself was supposed to have said, "My friend is my other self." In the event that two friends fought, the younger of the two was expected to apologize to the elder. Families were encouraged to live together harmoniously. Men and women were expected to choose their mates carefully and be faithful to one another. Pythagoras reasoned that more children meant that there would be more people to worship the gods, so students were encouraged to have children.

PYTHAGORAS'S FAMILY

The accounts of Pythagoras's life offer contradicting stories about his family. Most report that he married a woman named Theano, who was likely one of his disciples. Her father is believed to have been one of

THE DAILY ROUTINE

Considering how little we know about some Pythagorean teachings, it is remarkable how much we know about the society members' day-to-day lives. Disciples who lived full-time at Pythagoras's school experienced a regimented daily routine, beginning with lying in bed and thinking about the previous day's events, then mentally planning the day ahead. Once out of bed, a Pythagorean took a solitary walk, followed by socializing with others and making offerings to the gods at the temple. Initiates then went to the gymnasium for exercise. Afterward, they ate lunch, which consisted of bread and honey. Then, they took another walk, this time in groups of two or three, in which they discussed lessons. Baths came next. At night, students gathered in groups of about ten for dinner. The mealtime included readings, socializing, and religious rituals. Finally, students were encouraged to recall the day's events before falling asleep. Pythagoras encouraged this habit, as he believed that it enhanced memory, a capability that was crucial if a student was to be able to learn his complex and coded lessons.

Pythagoras's disciples, too. A treatise on the "golden ratio," also known as the "golden mean" has been ascribed to Theano. Many historians consider Theano to have been the first female mathematician.

Theano and Pythagoras are said to have had several children, but sources differ on how many and what their names were. The most commonly mentioned child of the pair was their daughter Damo, who became a prominent Pythagorean herself.

CHAPTER FOUR

PYTHAGOREAN BELIEFS

Pythagoras may have been the first man in history to refer to himself as a philosopher, which literally means "a lover of wisdom." To the Pythagoreans, the distinction between philosophy and religion was blurry. Their teachings regarding the human soul and religion were a combination of mystical beliefs and a more scientific pursuit of knowledge. Pythagoras was open to knowledge in any form it might take, including the religious traditions of many countries and cultures.

The fundamental principle in Pythagorean thought is the absolute belief in and reverence for numbers. To Pythagoras, numbers were the essence of all human knowledge and existence. It was only through the study of numbers that men and women could hope to understand the workings of the soul, as well as the universe around them. The Pythagoreans used numbers to create a model of the universe. They also used numbers to determine on which days they should worship in the temple. They believed that the world's secrets would be revealed to those who held the key, and that key was numbers.

We know surprisingly little about what Pythagoras actually taught in his school. The school's secrecy has made understanding Pythagorean teaching something of a scavenger hunt. Historians have pieced together information from the writings and teachings of the Pythagoreans who lived at least one generation after their master's death. Yet even with that information, it is difficult to say which teachings were Pythagoras's, which ones came from his Croton disciples, and which were those of the Pythagoreans who lived well after the community on Croton had ceased to exist.

Despite the lack of primary sources, the fundamentals of Pythagorean thought have survived through the centuries. To the Pythagoreans, all knowledge was broken down into four categories. The first, arithmetic, was the study

This relief shows a bull being sacrificed to Asclepius, the god of health. Temples dedicated to him doubled as the first hospitals, showing the fine line between religion and science at the time.

of mathematics. The second was music and harmony. The third was geometry, which included the study of the heavens, namely, cosmology and astronomy. The fourth and final area of study was philosophy.

It is important to keep in mind that in the ancient world, these four categories were not distinct areas of study. At almost every turn, these fields of study overlapped and often blended together. For example, the Pythagoreans' study of music was central to their study of geometry. Mathematics and religion were also a part of their musical and astronomical theories, as we will see. Keeping this in mind, it is time to take a closer

look at the wisdom that Pythagoras shared with his followers and that has been handed down to us today.

THE PYTHAGOREAN SOUL

Pythagoras believed that the soul was made of three essential parts: reason, emotion, and intelligence. In Pythagoras's native land of Samos, this three-part conception was the least controversial aspect of his theories regarding the soul. Pythagoras's travels in Egypt and the East had introduced him to concepts regarding the soul that were unfamiliar to the ancient Greeks. The Pythagoreans believed that the human soul was immortal and that upon death it transmigrated from one body to another. It is a belief similar to what we call reincarnation today. In addition, Pythagoras and his followers claimed that disembodied souls act as demons that harm a person's ability to function normally, through such harmful activities as possession.

Traditionally, the ancient Greeks believed that after death the soul was destined for Hades. Hades was the dark underworld of the dead. A mortal soul could never return from Hades. Once there, a soul was considered dead to the ancient Greeks. It was no longer part of the living world. Only an immortal, a god, could escape Hades. The Greeks were not receptive to Eastern beliefs about the transmigration of the soul. The Pythagoreans were often ridiculed for claiming that the soul was immortal and able to move from one body to another. Pythagoras, himself, was made fun of

The classical vision of Hades is pictured on this fourth-century-BCE vase from southern Italy. In the middle, Hades, king of the underworld, sits facing his queen, Persephone.

in particular for claiming to be able to recognize the souls of friends and family in their new bodies.

THE LIMITED AND THE UNLIMITED

One aspect of Pythagorean philosophy is the concept of limited and unlimited. Pythagoras believed that the world is made of these two essential elements. The limited represents the physical world and most of the things that people sense through taste, touch, hearing, seeing, and smelling. The unlimited is the world that humans cannot see or experience, the world of the gods and all things divine. The unlimited, according to Pythagoras, is the real world. The physical world, the limited, is only a temporary world that may be used until the unlimited becomes infinite. This dual concept of the world is still popular today. Many philosophers and theologians view the world as having two opposing aspects, usually in the form of the physical versus the spiritual, the mortal versus the immortal, the temporal versus the infinite.

The Pythagoreans believed in harmony as well as duality. They were not comfortable with the idea of a world in conflict. Pythagoras's followers believed that there was a way to bring the limited into harmony with the unlimited. As usual in Pythagorean thought, the answer lay in mathematics and music. To understand mathematics was to understand music. To understand both was thought to give people the ability to see the invisible workings of the unlimited.

THE GODS

Because the Pythagorean society on Croton was as much a religious community as it was a philosophical or mathematical one, the worship of the gods was central to the Pythagorean way of life. Above all, the Pythagoreans revered the Greek god Apollo, who was the god of the sun, music, art, medicine, prophecy, and philosophy. Given the

Here, Apollo is depicted standing between his mother, Leto, and his twin sister, Artemis. The stringed instrument he is playing, called a kithara, is part of the lyre family.

subjects that the Pythagoreans pursued—mathematics, music, geometry, and philosophy—it is not surprising that Apollo was a central figure of honor.

The Pythagoreans were very particular about the methods that they used for worshipping the gods. The rituals that they adopted were a combination of Greek and Egyptian religious practices. The Pythagoreans' belief in the sacredness of numbers also seems to have had an effect on their religious practices. The concept of the limited and unlimited played a role in religious worship, too. Pythagoras adopted key elements from Egyptian religious rituals, such as burning incense and herbs as sacrifices to the gods. Numbers determined the proper days on which to worship. All libations—sacrifices of liquids, such as wine—were made three times to mirror the utterances of the Pythian priestesses of the

Libations, usually of wine or olive oil, played a key role in Greek religion. This sketch based on an ancient vase shows a male figure holding a libation and sitting on a tripod.

Oracle of Delphi, who spoke their prophecies from tri-pods (three-legged stools).

Pythagoras urged his followers to enter temples on the right side, which they associated with the unlimited, and exit temples on the left, which they associated with the limited. According to Iamblichus, entering the temple represents entering the unlimited. Exiting it represents a return to the world of humans, the limited. Pythagoras urged his followers to keep the limited and unlimited sep-arate by not burning the bodies of the dead. As flames were considered sacred, it would be inappropriate to bring this divine, unlimited element into contact with a physical body, the ultimate symbol of the limited.

A REVERENCE FOR NUMBERS

Understanding the contributions that Pythagoras made to the science of mathematics and geometry begins with a look at something altogether less scientific—numerology. Numerology is the study of the supernatural power of num-bers and their supposed ability to influence events in people's lives. Pythagoras and his followers believed that numbers were not just symbols and existed independently of anything that they might represent. The Pythagoreans believed that numbers had personalities and characteristics.

Pythagoreans accepted only whole, positive num-bers as actual numbers. In other words, they did not deal with fractions, negative numbers, or even the number 0. They believed that odd numbers represented the unlim-ited, the world of the gods, the world that most people cannot see or even comprehend. Odd numbers also symbolized maleness, stillness, the right, and the good. Even numbers, on the other hand, represented the limited, the visible world of humans. For Pythagoras, even numbers also symbolized the female, motion, the left, darkness, and evil. Interestingly, the Pythagoreans considered the number 1 as both odd and even.

Pythagoras attributed very specific characteristics to certain numbers. He considered the first ten numbers sacred, with 10 being the most sacred of all. Each number was given a name and a set of defining properties.

The number 1, called the monad, was the origin of everything—the starting point of all life and other numbers. The monad was sacred because the Pythagoreans believed that it existed in every number, especially 2 through 10, the other sacred numbers. The monad number represented the divine to the Pythagoreans. It was the symbol of existence and being.

The number 2, called the dyad, represented creation. It embodied duality and opposites. The Pythagoreans considered it a daring number for having the courage to break away from the monad. The dyad could potentially express the conflict that arises from opposites.

The number 3, or the triad, was the first true number. It expressed a multitude, or many, and symbolized wholeness because it contains the beginning, the middle, and the end. To the Pythagoreans, the number 3 represented the soul, which they thought consisted of three parts: reason, emotion, and intelligence. The triad was also considered the symbol of matter, as matter is three-dimensional. Finally, the number 3 exemplified knowledge, a place of honor for the Pythagoreans, and therefore was thought of as the first true number. The Pythagoreans, who revered oracles, pointed out that the tripod used by the Pythian priestess had three legs.

The tetrad was the name given to the number 4. The tetrad represented completion. Four was the number of seasons in the year as well as the number of the four basic elements: earth, air, fire, and water. Four is a number associated with musical intervals, so the tetrad was also sacred in music. Finally, the tetrad was the number associated with planetary movement, which the Pythagoreans believed created musical sounds.

The number 5, named the pentad, was considered holy because it was the number that exemplified marriage and love. It stood for the coming together of opposites, in particular men and women. The Pythagoreans saw the number

Most marriages in ancient Greece were arranged. This vase shows a wedding procession, in which a bride is brought from her father's house to her husband's.

5 as the sum of the first even and odd number, 2 plus 3 (as 1 was neither exclusively odd or even, but both at the same time).

The next number, 6, or the hexad, as it was called, represented health to the Pythagoreans. It was the number of balance in the world. The Pythagoreans had a mathematical reason for this. First, the sum of the first three numbers—1, 2, and 3—equals 6. Also, if multiplied, these same three numbers again equal 6. For the Pythagoreans, who considered all things in the world fundamentally mathematical in nature, the fact that the sum and product of the first three numbers would yield the same number was evidence that the gods spoke in numbers. Therefore, the hexad held a place of honor among the sacred numbers.

The number 7, called the heptad, symbolized the human body because the head has seven openings (mouth, two nostrils, two ears, two eyes). Also, the body has seven

basic body parts: the head, the neck, the torso, two legs, and two arms. It expressed, too, the sacred musical instrument, the lyre, which had seven strings. The heptad was considered the fortress of numbers—7 cannot be divided by any number other than itself. Finally, it symbolized the Pythagoreans' seven basic ages of a human: infant, child, adolescent, young adult, adult, elder, and old person.

The octad was the name given to the number 8. It embodied friendship and steadfastness for Pythagoras's followers. It was the first number that was a cube—a number multiplied by itself, with the product again multiplied by that number. For example: 2 x 2 = 4 and 4 x 2 = 8. Eight was a sacred number musically because it is the basic number of all musical ratios.

The number 9 was associated with poetry, music, and dance because there were nine Muses in Greek mythology. The Muses were the personifications of the

The muses were named Euterpe, Terpsichore, Erato, Calliope, Clio, Melpomene, Polyhymnia, Urania, and Thalia. Each inspired work in a different area, such as tragedy or dance.

arts and sciences—astronomy, comedy, dancing, epic poetry, history, lyric poetry, music, sacred poetry, and tragedy. People believed that artists and thinkers were inspired by the nine Muses to do great work in their particular field. Also known as the ennead, 9 acted as the horizon or threshold to the most sacred of all numbers, 10. For this reason, the number 9 was also referred to as the Oceanus, as it symbolized crossings and passages. The ennead also represented the number of months in a pregnancy.

The number 10, which Pythagoras and his followers called the decad, was the most sacred number of all. It was the number of eternity and divinity. It was considered the number that held all of the forces of the world together. According to Pythagoras, ten was the number of spheres that floated in the heavens. As such, all other numbers circled around this sacred number. Ten was the sum of $1 + 2 + 3 + 4$, the four most sacred numbers coming before 10. One of the reasons that the Pythagoreans considered 1, 2, 3, and 4 sacred was because they represented the three basic musical ratios: 4:3, 3:2, and 2:1.

The decad was also embodied in the Pythagoreans' most sacred symbol, the tetractus. In the Pythagorean tradition, the tetractus was not written as we would write the number today. Instead it was noted by a series of dots in a triangular shape. The tetractus denoted $1 + 2 + 3 + 4 = 10$ and was the numerical model of the soul and the universe.

The Pythagoreans' belief in numerology may seem a bit unusual in the twenty-first century, but these mystical beliefs were very much a part of the sixth century BCE and were certainly a part of the education that Pythagoras received in Egypt and Babylon. Mysticism is the belief that the spiritual understanding of a subject is more important than what is experienced or observed. Pythagorean numerology was certainly part of a mystical tradition. Due to the mystical elements of Pythagoras's teaching, some historians have been ready to discredit him as a quack with little to offer in terms of real mathematics. Perhaps it would be more appropriate to see these numerological beliefs as the result of Pythagoras's passion for numbers, a passion that some say was the very start of mathematics as we know it today.

VISUALIZING MATHEMATICS

To the Pythagoreans, there was only one hope for understanding the world; that hope was mathematics. Numerology may have played a large role in their attempt to piece together how the world works, but rigorous scientific methods also played an important role. Philolaus, a Pythagorean who lived about a hundred years after Pythagoras, brought some of Pythagoras's mathematical theories to the forefront. The Pythagoreans' study of numbers yielded some of the first genuine mathematical and geometrical theories in Western thought.

The way in which Pythagoras and his followers conceived of numbers was very different from the way mathematics is practiced today. In addition to representing quantities, numbers symbolized geometrical shapes.

Therefore, the Pythagoreans' study of geometry was linked closely to the study of mathematics. Today, numbers are portrayed by symbols. The concept of the number two, for instance, is written as the numeral 2. Pythagoreans used a much more ancient form of writing to represent numbers. Pythagorean mathematicians represented numbers by a series of equidistant (equally spaced) dots that formed lines, triangles, rectangles, and so forth (see figure 1). These numbers look very much like the markings found on dice or dominoes. In this way, Pythagoreans were able to see and change the shape of every number.

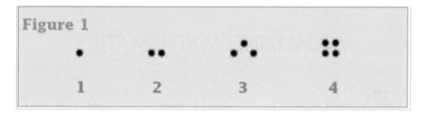

Figure 1

1   2   3   4

The Pythagoreans placed their most important numbers into four basic categories: triangles, squares, rectangles, and gnomons. Triangular numbers include any number that can be shaped into a triangle, using a series of dots. The numbers 3 and 10 (see figure 2) are examples of triangular numbers.

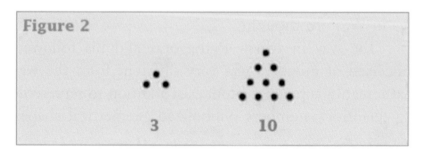

Figure 2

3   10

Square numbers are those that can be shaped into a square. Examples include the numbers 4 and 9 (see figure 3).

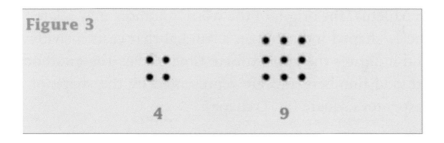

Figure 3

4   9

Take a closer look at the numbers 4 and 9. Their dots form squares, and these numbers are, indeed, what today we call square numbers. Four is the square of 2 (the product of a number multiplied by itself; 2 x 2 = 4), just as 9 is the square of 3 (3 x 3 = 9). The Pythagoreans did not just call these numbers squares; they actually visualized and wrote them as squares. Their system of representation using dots made the geometric properties of numbers easier to understand.

The next set of numbers in the Pythagorean system of categorization was the oblong numbers. Oblong numbers are best understood as being rectangular in shape. Examples of these rectangular numbers include the numbers 2, 6, and 8 (see figure 4).

Figure 4

2   6   8

Finally there is the group called the gnomons. Gnomon was the name of the sundial of Babylonian origin first used in Greece by Anaximander, Pythagoras's teacher in Miletus. The origin of the word "gnomon" may relate to the L-shaped indicator on a sundial that casts a shadow and indicates the approximate time of day. The gnomons are odd numbers and are represented by the shape of a carpenter's square (an L shape).

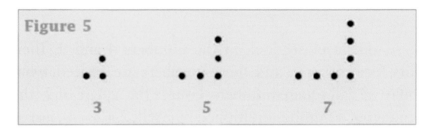

Figure 5

3   5   7

This method of representing and categorizing numbers is often seen as the very beginning of modern mathematics. Using this system, the Pythagoreans were able to manipulate numbers in a variety of ways. For example, they proposed that any two successive triangular numbers make a square number, and then they demonstrated the theory using their system of numerical representation. As shown in figure 6 below, when two consecutive triangular numbers, such as 3 and 6, are added together, they make a square number, 9.

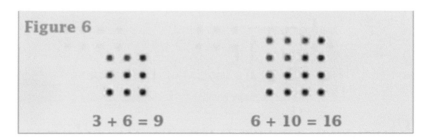

Figure 6

3 + 6 = 9   6 + 10 = 16

THE FAMOUS THEOREM

All of this tinkering with numbers and their shapes seemed bound to result in at least a few groundbreaking mathematical theories. Today most people associate Pythagoras with a single mathematical theorem that now bears his name—the Pythagorean theorem. The Pythagorean theorem states that in a right triangle—a triangle that has a 90-degree angle—the sum of the squares of the lengths of the two shorter sides equals the square of the length of the longest side. No student escapes an introduction to geometry course without learning that Pythagoras was the first to pronounce officially that $a^2 + b^2 = c^2$. But was Pythagoras truly the originator of this theorem?

Today, historians know that Pythagoras and his followers were not the first to make use of this theorem. There is some evidence that the Egyptians made use of it for many centuries before the Pythagoreans. Archaeologists have found cuneiform tablets suggesting that the Babylonians knew of the Pythagorean theorem as early as 1800 BCE. Milesian philosophers, including Pythagoras's teachers, Thales and Anaximander, were familiar with Babylonian science. Some historians believe that Pythagoras learned about the theorem while studying with these men. Scientists have also found evidence that the people of India and China knew about the theorem as far back as 500 BCE. One modern historian has even suggested that the theorem should be named the pre-Pythagorean theorem.

Does this mean that Pythagoras should not take credit for the theorem $a^2 + b^2 = c^2$? A closer look at the work that the Pythagoreans did with this theorem brings to light why it has become so closely associated with them. Pythagoras and his followers may not have been the first to make use of the theorem, but they were the first to attempt to explain it scientifically.

A right triangle is one in which two of the triangle's sides are perpendicular to each other, forming a right, or 90-degree, angle. The Pythagorean theorem states that with a right triangle, the sum of the squares of the lengths of the two shorter sides of the triangle equals the square of the length of the longest side. The hypotenuse, or the longest side, gets its name from two Greek words—*hypo*, meaning "below," and *tenuse*, meaning "stretch." The longest line in a right triangle is the line that stretches opposite the right angle.

Today's mathematical methods lead us to think of the Pythagorean theorem in strictly numerical terms. When we say $a^2 + b^2 = c^2$, we imagine multiplying *a* by *a* and adding that to *b* multiplied by *b*. This sum would be the same number as *c* multiplied by *c*. The Pythagoreans would be more likely to explain the theorem in the following way: the square built on the hypotenuse is equal to the sum of the squares built on the two shorter sides of the right triangle. Diagram 7 shows what the Pythagoreans meant when they talked about building the square on the lines of the triangle.

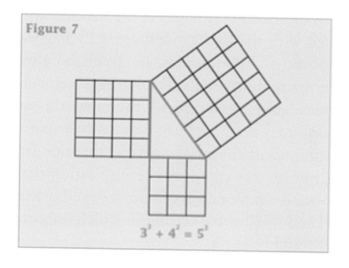

Figure 7

$$3^2 + 4^2 = 5^2$$

SQUARE NUMBERS AND MORE

In addition to the Pythagorean theorem, Pythagoras is credited with six other mathematical theorems. One of these is the theorem that states that eight triangular numbers (made up of the same number of dots) plus 1 equals a square number. As the diagram below shows, this theorem could also be demonstrated visually.

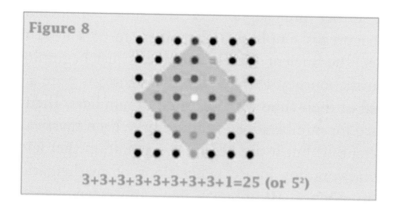

Figure 8

3+3+3+3+3+3+3+1=25 (or 5²)

It is difficult to say whether the mathematical work associated with the Pythagoreans was Pythagoras's own or the work of his disciples, or a collaborative effort between master and pupils. The Pythagorean community's secrecy has made it difficult to answer this question. Pythagoras may not have been personally responsible for discovering all of the mathematical theories attributed to him, but he was certainly the inspiration that led to this innovative exploration of numbers and provided the physical and intellectual setting in which important discoveries could be made.

The most important aspect of Pythagorean mathematics is not the actual mathematical discoveries that the group made as much as the philosophy behind its study of numbers. The Pythagoreans were the first group of people who tried to explain the world by using numbers. This is exactly what most scientists do today. Although their mathematical theories were often incorrect, the Pythagoreans were on the right track. Their mistakes helped those who came later discover some of the mathematical truths for which the Pythagoreans had been searching.

Other philosophers of the time considered the Pythagoreans' emphasis on numbers to be a little ridiculous. The ancient Greek world was just beginning its scientific journey. Perhaps the Pythagoreans were a little ahead of their time when it came to numbers. Their reverence for numbers may at times have been mystical and unscientific, but it did begin an exploration that laid the groundwork for future generations of mathematicians, not to mention astronomers, geographers, engineers, and other scientists who would remake the world and our understanding of it.

STUDYING THE SKIES

One of the key areas of study for the Pythagoreans was heavenly bodies. As with every other subject that they investigated, their ideas regarding the heavens were a mix of religious beliefs and hard science. Cosmology is the study of the origin and nature of the universe. It is a subject that tends to be speculative (involving mystical beliefs rather than direct, empirical observation). Astronomy, on the other hand, is the more scientific attempt to study the behavior of matter in outer space. Pythagoras's theories and observations about Earth, the sun, and the planets were a combination of these two fields. As with Pythagorean mathematics, much of what we know about the group's cosmological and astronomical work comes from Philolaus.

The Pythagoreans believed they had achieved a complete understanding of the creation and structure of the universe. According to Pythagoras's conception, the universe was made of ten spheres. These ten spheres were the sun, the moon, Earth, the five additional known planets at the time—Mercury, Venus, Mars, Jupiter, and Saturn—the counter-Earth, and the central hearth. Two of these bodies, the counter-Earth and the central hearth, were not observable in space.

According to Pythagorean cosmology, the central hearth lay at the very center of the universe and was the

Zeus, seen here with his wife, Hera, was the ruler of the gods. Zeus was also the god of the skies and weather; in particular he was associated with thunder and lightning.

origin of all of the other spheres. It was referred to as "the guard post of Zeus." Zeus was the leader of the Olympian gods (the twelve major gods of ancient Greek religion, who, as a group, take their name from Mount Olympus, where Zeus ruled with his wife, Hera). The Pythagoreans believed that the central hearth was the starting point of the universe and that it provided life and light to the world. Earth rotated around the hearth. Whether Earth was facing the hearth or not determined day or night.

The counter-Earth was a planetary sphere that, according to the Pythagoreans, was never visible from Earth because it lay on the other side of the central hearth. Aristotle accused the Pythagoreans of making up the counter-Earth simply so that there would be ten heavenly bodies instead of nine, making the number fit neatly into their numerological system. The number 10 was sacred to the Pythagoreans, and the idea of ten heavenly bodies may have been so irresistible to Pythagoras that he simply created a fictional sphere to reach that number.

Music and numbers were central to the Pythagoreans' cosmology. Pythagoras believed that the planets, the sun, and the moon all moved around the central hearth according to musical ratios. They believed that this planetary movement created musical sounds. Although most men and women could not hear this music, Pythagoras claimed that he could. The Pythagoreans believed that the faster a planet moved, the higher the pitch it made while in orbit around the central hearth. The slower-moving planets created lower-pitched music. Historians credit Pythagoras with being the first person to use the word *kosmos* to refer to the universe. *Kosmos* was a Greek word meaning "harmony." He used this word, which is the root of our words "cosmos" and "cosmology," because he believed that all things in the world, the heavenly bodies in particular, move harmoniously with one another.

As with their mathematics, the Pythagoreans' cosmology and astronomy were a mix of science and religious beliefs. While the central hearth and counter-Earth, along with the music of the planets, may have been mystical constructions on the part of Pythagoras, there are aspects of Pythagorean astronomy that demonstrate a more scientific approach to the study of the heavens.

The Pythagoreans were the first to claim that Earth was not the center of the universe. They believed, instead, that it rotated around a central point, the central hearth. Although they were mistaken about the central point (it is actually the sun), the notion that Earth behaved similarly to other planets in revolving around a central point was revolutionary. In addition, the Pythagoreans believed Earth to be round and suspended in space. During the sixth century BCE, most people believed that the world was flat or that it floated on a vast sea. This new idea was a clear departure from traditional thinking. Pythagoras's astronomical theories extended even to the scientific observation of the morning and evening star. He is credited as the first person to realize that these two stars were the same body. The morning and evening stars are, in fact, the planet Venus.

MUSIC AND MUSICAL THEORY

The Pythagoreans made substantial contributions to the field of musical theory. As was typical of Pythagoras and his followers, their examination of the structure and

The kithara was closely associated with Apollo, who is shown playing one on this kylix, or drinking cup. The kithara had more strings and was harder to play than a simple lyre.

nature of music combined religious and mystical beliefs with more scientific approaches.

For the Pythagoreans, music was a key element in both everyday and spiritual life. They believed that music had the power to heal a number of physical and mental ailments. They thought that good health depended on the selection of appropriate music. Pythagoras claimed that string instruments had healing powers, but that under no circumstances were his followers to use wind instruments for this purpose. Pythagoras found the sound of wind instruments to be unhelpful and even aggravating to the soul. The Pythagoreans prescribed specific tunes

SOOTHING THE SAVAGE BEAST

The Pythagoreans were convinced of the power of music. One Pythagorean legend tells how music played a crucial role in a military battle. Croton's neighboring city-state Sybaris had a very powerful cavalry numbering five thousand, which was preparing to attack Croton. The horses of this strong cavalry were trained to parade to music. The Crotonians called on Pythagoras for help. Pythagoras and his disciples played tunes that mesmerized the horses into dancing rather than attacking. With Sybaris's cavalry prancing and high-stepping rather than charging, Croton was able to win the battle.

and dances to cure conditions such as rage, anger, and sadness. Pythagoras even asked his followers to listen to specific songs in the morning to help them wake up and start the day off well. He prescribed a different type of music for falling asleep at night.

Music was also central to the Pythagoreans' religious practices. They worshipped Apollo, the god of music, and were dedicated to Orpheus, the legendary poet and musician who features in several Greek myths. They integrated music, poetry, and dance into their religious ceremonies. Unfortunately, none of the

Orpheus visited the underworld in an attempt to bring his wife, Eurydice, back to life. This relief shows the couple with Hermes, the god who guided souls to the underworld.

Pythagorean tunes survived, so the sound of their music has been lost to the ages.

For Pythagoras and his followers, music and mathematics were inseparable. It was the combination of these two elements that allowed people to understand the unlimited concept of the universe. The Pythagoreans thought music was the manifestation of harmony in the world. They believed that for those who possessed a certain kind of knowledge, the musical harmony of the world could be heard, especially in the movement of the planets.

But what did Pythagoras mean when he said that music and mathematics were closely related to one another? The answer to this question is well illustrated by the story of Pythagoras's discovery of musical ratios. According to tradition, Pythagoras was strolling by a blacksmith's shop when he realized that the sound of pounding hammers was creating a musical sound. Curious, he went into the shop and inquired about the hammers the blacksmith used. As the story goes, the hammers' weight ratios were six, eight, nine, and twelve. Upon learning this, Pythagoras returned to

Pythagoras's musical ideas shaped Western music for millennia. This woodcut, published in Naples in 1480, is one of a series showing Pythagoras's experiments with the harmonic scale.

his community and began experimenting with an instrument called a monochord (so named because it only has one string). By dividing the one string on the monochord at different places and then plucking it, the Pythagoreans were able to begin their experiments with musical ratios.

According to Pythagoras, the ratios of the blacksmith's weights when applied to the monochord's string created the same musical consonance that he had heard coming from the blacksmith's pounding hammers. A musical consonance is a combination of sounds that occur at the same time that many people consider harmonious and pleasing to the human ear. When sounded simultaneously, Pythagoras's humming strings demonstrated that certain ratios created pleasing sounds. Using the humming string of the monochord, Pythagoras was able to name three musical ratios that musicians continue to use today. They are the ratio 2:1, which represents a musical octave; 3:2, which represents a musical fifth; and 4:3, which represents a musical fourth. How do these ratios correspond to the blacksmith's hammers? The hammers weighed 6, 8, 9, and 12 pounds (2.7, 3.6, 4.1, 5.4 kilograms). When the ratio 12:6 is simplified, it becomes 2:1. Similarly, 9:6 is the same as 3:2, and 8:6 is 4:3. To the spiritually minded Pythagoreans, the fact that the three musical ratios that they discovered included only the sacred numbers 1, 2, 3, and 4 was nothing short of miraculous. In addition, these four numbers added up to 10, the mystical tetractus. They considered it just one more indication that the world was arranged according to numbers.

Since Pythagoras's lifetime, many more musical ratios have been discovered, but the Pythagoreans were the first to make the direct connection between music and numbers. Given their groundbreaking work with music, it is not surprising that the work of Pythagoras and his followers is considered the foundation upon which all Western music theory is based. As with numbers, the Pythagoreans' religious beliefs and practices resulted in discoveries that were as much a part of the realm of science as they were of faith.

CHAPTER FIVE

A LASTING LEGACY

T hough Pythagoras died roughly two and a half millennia ago, the influence of the Pythagoreans can still be seen today. This is particularly impressive given the complete absence of primary-source documents and the fact that many of the secondary documents that do survive paint Pythagoras as a near-legendary figure. The persistence of Pythagorean thought in the year following Pythagoras's death is itself impressive, especially given the violent opposition the movement faced near the end of Pythagoras's own life.

PYTHAGORAS IN EXILE

Unfortunately for Pythagoras and his followers, the society they had created in Croton did not last for more than a few decades. The stable and prosperous colony that Pythagoras had chosen for his school had grown in power and wealth, but not all of its citizens were happy with its government. They were particularly angry at the strong influence that the Pythagoreans had on the ruling class, which held most of the power in Croton.

During the school's existence, the Pythagoreans' sway over the colony's government had steadily grown. The rulers of Croton were a small group of aristocrats, many of whom were followers of Pythagoras. As political instability grew in Croton, so did the average Crotonian's resentment of Pythagoras's influence on their government. The people's distrust of the Pythagorean community was in part due to the school's secretiveness. Here was a group that did not reveal any of its teachings yet played a major political role in people's lives.

People opposed to Pythagoras's influence decided it was time to rid Croton of the philosopher and his followers. Some accounts say that Cylon, a wealthy nobleman of Croton who had been refused membership in the society due to his violent tendencies and unpleasant personality, became the leader of the anti-Pythagorean faction. The Crotonians decided that the Pythagoreans must be expelled from Croton. Their methods were violent and effective. During a large indoor meeting of the Pythagorean community, the opponents burned down the building in which the group had gathered. Pythagoras was one of the few who survived. After the slaughter in Croton, Pythagoras retired from public life. However, the persecution of the Pythagoreans did not stop. They were chased throughout southern Italy. Even non-members who sympathized with them were persecuted and killed.

The details of Pythagoras's death are not clear. Some historians believe that he spent some time moving from one southern Italian colony to another, trying to stay one step ahead of those who wanted to kill him. According to tradition, Pythagoras sought refuge in the Temple of the Muses in the southern Italian colony of Metapontum. His attackers did not dare to go into such a sacred place to kill him, but neither did they allow any of his supporters to enter in order to assist him. Pythagoras, cut off from outside supplies, eventually died of starvation in the temple.

After Pythagoras's death, his followers spread out from Italy into Sicily and Greece. A generation later, some of the Pythagoreans returned to Croton and reestablished the school that their master had founded. The new school in Croton lasted until about 300 BCE. Aristaeus, a close disciple of Pythagoras's, may have taken over as the society's leader and even married Pythagoras's widow.

PYTHAGORAS INSPIRES OTHERS

Before Pythagoras died, many philosophers and mathematicians knew of his ideas. But after his death and the destruction of his society, Pythagoras's ideas spread even wider and faster. Some saw the Pythagoreans as an extreme group of religious fanatics and attempted to discredit them and their teachings. Others looked past their strange, secretive way of life to discover the practical value of their theories regarding numbers, music, and astronomy.

Plato is perhaps the best-known and most respected name in ancient Greek philosophy. One of Plato's mentors was a Pythagorean from Sicily named Archytas. Considered the first master mathematician in the Pythagorean tradition,

SOURCES ON PYTHAGORAS

The most extensive sources on Pythagoras's life and philosophy are Iamblichus's *On the Pythagorean Life*, Porphyry's *Life of Pythagoras*, and Diogenes Laertius's *Life of Pythagoras*, all of which date from the third century ce. All three build on or quote fragments of earlier sources, many of which are now lost but none of which dated back as far as Pythagoras himself.

Both Iamblichus and Porphyry were neo-Platonists and almost certainly attributed later philosophers' ideas to Pythagoras in their attempts to claim him as the original Greek philosopher. The biographer Diogenes Laertius, though more objective in some respects, does rely on some pseudo-Pythagorean texts, or forged texts that purported to be the work of Pythagoras or other Pythagoreans.

Archytas's influence on Plato is unmistakable. In Plato's most scientific work, *Timaeus*, he claims that musical ratios guide heavenly bodies, a belief traced directly back to Pythagoras. Additionally, Plato's belief in a visible and an invisible world mirrors the Pythagorean conception of limited and unlimited worlds.

By the second century CE, all of the Pythagorean societies had vanished. The Roman philosophers, however, revived Pythagorean thought. They closely associated Pythagorean thought with Plato's ideas, which were also in the midst of a revival. During this period, the neo-Platonic and neo-Pythagorean traditions became blended, so much so that it is difficult to tell one from the other.

Throughout the Middle Ages, Pythagoras continued to be a revered figure, though during this time almost all of the knowledge that scholars had about Pythagoras came from neo-Pythagorean writers. The Roman writer Boethius's descriptions of Pythagorean teachings in his *De Institutione Arithmetica and De Institutione Musica* were particularly influential. It was Boethius who introduced the Latin term *quadrivium* ("four roads"). Medieval universities taught both the *trivium* ("three roads," which consisted of grammar, logic, and rhetoric) and the more advanced quadrivium (arithmetic, geometry, music, and astronomy). While the trivium-quadrivium system does not break down subjects in the same way the Pythagoreans did, it does place topics that the Pythagoreans focused on at the top of its hierarchy of knowledge.

Pythagorean ideas were also important to medieval music and music theory. Pythagorean tuning, based

Later writers saw Pythagoras as a major influence on Plato, seen in this Roman copy of a Greek bust. However, Plato made few references to Pythagoras in his own writings.

on the Pythagorean scale, was widely used in medieval music. Stories of Pythagoras's musical experiments, both with hammers and bells and with the monochord, were widely known and there are a number of illustrations of them in manuscripts from the era.

Even after the Middle Ages gave way to the Renaissance, Pythagoras remained an inspiration. The Italian scholar Marsilio Ficino—famous for translating the works of Plato into Latin, introducing the Latin-speaking scholars of Western Europe to texts that had not been available to them during the Middle Ages—also translated works of several neo-Platonists and neo-Pythagoreans, including several pseudo-Pythagorean texts and works by Porphyry and Iamblichus.

Pythagorean ideas inspired astronomers of the Renaissance, too. In 1530, Polish-born Nicolaus Copernicus (1473–1543), the first modern astronomer, claimed that the sun was at the center of our universe and that Earth rotated around the sun. In making this claim, Copernicus contradicted the prevailing view at the time that Earth was the center of the universe around which everything else revolved. To escape punishment from religious authorities who insisted that God had made Earth and man the center of the universe, Copernicus did not publish his findings until soon before his death. Today, the Copernican system is widely accepted. In his writings, Copernicus expresses gratitude to Pythagoras for laying the groundwork for his astronomical discovery.

German astronomer Johannes Kepler (1571–1630) also credited Pythagoras as an inspiration for his many

Kepler's 1619 book, Harmonices Mundi *(in English:* The harmony of the world)*, united music, astronomy, and geometry in a Pythagorean manner but also disproved certain Pythagorean claims.*

discoveries in mathematics and astronomy. During the sixteenth century, Kepler proved that Copernicus had been correct—Kepler's laws of planetary motion show the sun to be the center of the universe. Kepler even went so far as to call himself a Pythagorean, because he, like Pythagoras, believed that a divine being created the universe according to mathematical principles.

Pythagoras's work in other areas continued to inspire as well. Pythagorean ideas about music led Sir Isaac Newton (1642–1727), the famous Enlightenment scientist and philosopher, to credit him with discovering musical ratios. In fact, Newton began to associate his own theory of gravity with Pythagoras. This gave Pythagoras credit for a discovery he actually had nothing to do with, but suggesting it shows the esteem in which Newton held him.

PYTHAGORAS TODAY

Today, Pythagoras is remembered primarily as a mathematician. However, his influence also extends to current religious beliefs. The ideas he formulated concerning the soul's immortality and transmigration influenced thinkers from Plato to modern-day spiritualists.

Despite Pythagoras's influential legacy in a variety of fields, he remains a mysterious, poorly understood figure. Today's scholars are still debating whether Pythagoras was one of the very first true scientists or simply a religious fanatic who happened to have some insight into mathematics and music and made a few lucky guesses about the nature of the universe. Scholars question whether Pythagoras is even responsible for the ideas and discoveries attributed to him. Given the scarcity of primary sources, historians may never answer these questions satisfactorily. Perhaps they do not need to be answered.

The clear distinction drawn between science and faith during the twenty-first century might have appeared strange and unnatural to Pythagoras, who saw no contradiction or seam between the two. His faith in numbers and their harmonious ordering of the universe led Pythagoras to investigations that changed the way future generations perceived the world. We have Pythagoras to thank for introducing us to the awe-inspiring power of numbers.

TIMELINE

CIRCA 569 BCE Pythagoras is born on the island of Samos. His father is Mnesarchus of Tyre, a merchant. His mother is Parthenis, a Samos native. In his youth, he is taught by the philosopher Pherecydes on the island of Syros.

CIRCA 550 BCE Pythagoras travels to Miletus and studies under the famous and respected philosophers Thales and Anaximander. In Miletus, Pythagoras is probably instructed in mathematics, astronomy, geometry, and cosmology.

CIRCA 535 BCE Following the advice of Thales, Pythagoras journeys to Egypt and becomes influenced by Egyptian spiritual traditions and practices and is eventually accepted into the priesthood.

525 BCE Cambyses II, king of Persia, invades Egypt. Pythagoras is taken prisoner and exiled to Babylon, where he studies under Persian magi and learns their sacred rites and mystical traditions. He also studies math and music there.

CIRCA 520 BCE Pythagoras gains his freedom and leaves Babylon, eventually returning to Samos and founding his school, the Semicircle.

CIRCA 518 BCE Pythagoras leaves Samos and travels to southern Italy, where he eventually founds a religious and philosophical society at Croton.

CIRCA 495 BCE The Pythagorean society at Croton comes under attack. Pythagoras escapes, possibly to Metapontum, where he is said to have died. Some accounts suggest he killed himself in despair over the destruction of his society in Croton. Another account reports that he sought refuge in Metapontum's Temple of the Muses and starved to death there. Other accounts claim that Pythagoras failed to escape Croton and was killed there. One tradition insists that he actually returned to Croton and lived to be about one hundred years old.

CIRCA 460 BCE After becoming more and more political in nature and splitting into several factions, meeting houses of the Pythagorean society throughout Italy, including in Croton, are attacked and burned. The society itself is suppressed and outlawed.

GLOSSARY

COLONY In the ancient world, a city-state that was founded by people from a mother city, with which it maintained important ties.

COMMUNAL Characterized by shared owner-ship and use of property or shared experiences and responsibilities in a domestic setting.

COSMOLOGY The study of the origin, history, and dynamics of the universe.

CUNEIFORM Characters formed by the arrangement of small, wedge-shaped elements and used in ancient Sumerian, Assyrian, Baby-lonian, and Persian writing.

DUALITY The state or condition of having two, often opposite, parts or elements.

EMPIRICISM The position that all knowledge is gained through the experience of the senses.

EXILE A period of forced or voluntary absence from one's country or home.

FUNDAMENTALS The first principles or most basic elements of something.

HYPOTENUSE The side of a right triangle opposite the right angle.

INFINITE Endless; without limit; eternal.

INITIATION The rites and ceremonies by which one is made a member of a club or society.

LIBATION A liquid that is poured out as a religious offering.

LYRE A stringed instrument of the harp family that has two curved arms connected at the upper end by a crossbar, used primarily in ancient Greece.

MAGI Babylonian wise men, part of Persia's priest caste.

MYSTICISM The belief that spiritual knowledge can be gained through insight or intuition.

NOVICE A new or inexperienced member of a group.

NUMEROLOGY The study of the supposed hidden influence of numbers on human affairs.

ORACLE A person (usually a priest or priestess in ancient tradition) through whom God or the gods are thought to speak; the shrine in which a deity reveals hidden wisdom through a person.

PYTHIAN PRIESTESSES Priestesses who served at the Oracle of Delphi and, under the influence of divine inspiration, answered the questions of those who came to honor the god Apollo.

REVERENCE A deep and solemn respect for something.

TEMPORAL Relating to time (as opposed to eternity) and earthly life.

TENET A principle or belief, especially a religious or philosophical one.

THEOLOGIAN A person who studies the nature of the divine.

THEOREM A mathematical statement that can be proven based on statements that were previously proven.

TRANSMIGRATION The movement of the soul from one body to another after death.

FOR MORE INFORMATION

American Mathematical Society

201 Charles Street

Providence, RI 02904

(800) 321-4267

Website: http://www.ams.org

Founded in 1881, this group promotes mathematical research and education, supports those in the profession of mathematics, and encourages an appreciation of mathematics. Along with its headquarters in Providence, the group also has offices in Washington, D.C., and Ann Arbor, Michigan.

American Philosophical Society

104 South Fifth Street

Philadelphia, PA 19106

(215) 440-3400, extension 4267

Website: http://www.amphilsoc.org

The American Philosophical Society has been an important force in American intellectual life since it was founded in 1743. As founder Benjamin Franklin put it, the society's aim is "promoting useful knowledge."

American School of Classical Studies in Athens

54 Souedias Street

GR-106 76 Athens

Greece

Website: http://www.ascsa.edu.gr

This home base for American scholars and students studying Greek history and culture in Greece itself was founded in 1881. The school's libraries are world renowned, but the school is probably best known for the many archaeological excavations it has sponsored.

Ancient Philosophy Society

240 Sparks Avenue

University Park, PA 16802

(800) 444-2419

Website: http://www.ancientphilosophysociety.org

The APS was founded in 1999 to "provide a forum for diverse scholarship on ancient Greek and Roman texts." It holds an annual meeting and has a website that features reading recommendations from members.

Canadian Mathematical Society

209 - 1725 St. Laurent Boulevard

Ottawa, ON K1G 3V4

Canada

Website: https://cms.math.ca

The goal of this organization, founded in 1945 as the Canadian Mathematical Congress, is to "promote and advance the discovery, learning and application of mathematics." Among other activities, it hosts the Canadian Mathematical Olympiad, a prestigious competition for college students.

Canadian Philosophical Association

P.O. Box 47077; rpo Blackburn Hamlet

Gloucester, ON K1B 5P9

Canada

(613) 236-1393, extension 2454

Website: http://www.acpcpa.ca/en

This group was founded in 1958 to further the cause of philosophical education and scholarship in Canada. The association publishes a quarterly journal, called *Dialogue*, and makes a point of carrying out all its business bilingually, in both English and French.

National Museum of Mathematics

11 East 26th Street

New York, NY 10010

(212) 542-0566

Website: http://momath.org

This museum is aimed particularly at children and teens. Its goal is to expand the public's understanding and appreciation of mathematics. It has exhibits and a full slate of activities to engage visitors.

WEBSITES

Because of the changing nature of Internet links, Rosen Publishing has developed an online list of websites related to the subject of this book. This site is updated regularly. Please use this link to access the list:

http://www.rosenlinks.com/GGP/Pyth

For Further Reading

Cohen, Marc S., Patricia Curd, and C. D. C. Reeve. *Readings in Ancient Greek Philosophy: From Thales to Aristotle.* 4th ed. Indianapolis, IN: Hackett Publishing Company, Inc., 2011.

Crease, Robert P. *The Great Equations: Breakthroughs in Science from Pythagoras to Heisenberg.* New York, NY: W. W. Norton & Company, 2010.

El Koussa, Karim. *Pythagoras the Mathemagician.* Mechanicsburg, PA: Sunbury Press, Inc., 2010.

Ferguson, Kitty. *The Music of Pythagoras: How an Ancient Brotherhood Cracked the Code of the Universe and Lit the Path from Antiquity to Outer Space.* New York, NY: Walker & Company, 2008.

Guthrie, Kenneth Sylvan, comp. and trans. *The Pythagorean Sourcebook and Library: An Anthology of Ancient Writings Which Relate to Pythagoras and Pythagorean Philosophy.* Grand Rapids, MI: Phanes Press, 1987.

Heller-Roazen, Daniel. *The Fifth Hammer: Pythagoras and the Disharmony of the World.* Brooklyn, NY: Zone Books, 2011.

Joost-Gaugier, Christiane L. *Pythagoras and Renaissance Europe: Finding Heaven.* New York, NY: Cambridge University Press, 2014.

Kahn, Charles H. *Pythagoras and the Pythagoreans: A Brief History.* Indianapolis, IN: Hackett Publishing Company, Inc., 2001.

Kaplan, Robert, and Ellen Kaplan. *Hidden Harmonies: The Lives and Times of the Pythagorean Theorem.* New York, NY: Bloomsbury Press, 2011.

Martinez, Alberto A. *The Cult of Pythagoras: Math and Myths.* Pittsburgh, PA: University of Pittsburgh Press, 2013.

Mazur, Joseph. *Enlightening Symbols: A Short History of Mathematical Notation and Its Hidden Powers.* Princeton, NJ: Princeton University Press, 2014.

McKirahan, Richard D. *Philosophy Before Socrates: An Introduction with Texts and Commentary.* Indianapolis, IN: Hackett Publishing Company, Inc., 2011.

Parker, Robert. *On Greek Religion* (Cornell Studies in Classical Philology). Ithaca, NY: Cornell University Press, 2011.

Reimer, David. *Count Like an Egyptian: A Hands-on Introduction to Ancient Mathematics.* Princeton, NJ: Princeton University Press, 2014.

Rudman, Peter S. *The Babylonian Theorem: The Mathematical Journey to Pythagoras and Euclid.* Amherst, NY: Prometheus Books, 2010.

Sangalli, Arturo. *Pythagoras' Revenge: A Mathematical Mystery.* Princeton, NJ: Princeton University Press, 2011.

Stamatellos, Giannis. *Introduction to Presocratics: A Thematic Approach to Early Greek Philosophy with Key Readings.* Hoboken, NJ: Wiley-Blackwell, 2012.

Uzdavinys, Algis. *The Golden Chain: An Anthology of Pythagorean and Platonic Philosophy* (Treasures of the World's Religions). Bloomington, IN: World Wisdom, 2004.

Warrior, Valerie. *Greek Religion: A Sourcebook.* Indianapolis, IN: Focus Classical Sources, 2009.

Waterfield, Robin. *The First Philosophers: The Presocratics and Sophists* (Oxford World's Classics). New York, NY: Oxford University Press, 2009.

BIBLIOGRAPHY

Brunschwig, Jaques, and Geoffrey E. R. Lloyd, eds. *A Guide to Greek Thought: Major Figures and Trends.* Cambridge, MA: Belknap Press of Harvard University Press, 2003.

Bunson, Margaret R. *Encyclopedia of Ancient Egypt* (Facts on File Library of World History). New York, NY: Facts on File, 2009.

Department of Ancient Near Eastern Art, the Metropolitan Museum of Art. "The Phoenicians." *Heilbrunn Timeline of Art History.* Retrieved December 12, 2014 (http://www.metmuseum .org/toah/hd/phoe/hd_phoe.htm).

Ellis, Julie. *What's Your Angle, Pythagoras?* Watertown, MA: Charlesbridge Publishing, 2004.

Ferguson, Kitty. *The Music of Pythagoras: How an Ancient Brotherhood Cracked the Code of the Universe and Lit the Path from Antiquity to Outer Space.* New York, NY: Walker & Company, 2008.

Godwin, Joscelyn. *The Harmony of the Spheres: A Sourcebook of the Pythagorean Tradition in Music.* Rochester, VT: Inner Traditions International, 1993.

Greaves, Alan M. *The Land of Ionia: Society and Economy in the Archaic Period.* Hoboken, NJ: Wiley-Blackwell, 2010.

Guthrie, Kenneth Sylvan. *The Pythagorean Source-book and Library: An Anthology of Ancient Writings Which Relate to Pythagoras and Pythagorean Philosophy.* Grand Rapids, MI: Phanes Press, 1987.

Kahn, Charles H. *Pythagoras and the Pythagoreans: A Brief History.* Indianapolis, IN: Hackett Publishing Company, Inc., 2001.

Mankiewicz, Richard. *The Story of Mathematics.* Princeton, NJ: Princeton University Press, 2000.

Strohmeier, John, and Peter Westbrook. *Divine Harmony: The Life and Teachings of Pythagoras.* Berkeley, CA: Berkeley Hill Books, 1999.

Taylor, Thomas, trans. *Iamblichus' Life of Pythagoras.* Rochester, VT: Inner Traditions International, 1986.

Valens, Evans G. *The Number of Things: Pythagoras, Geometry, and Humming Strings.* New York, NY: Dutton, 1964.

INDEX

S

Samos, 9–10, 37, 52
    Pythagoras's problems in, 31, 33–34
    Pythagoras's return to, 30–31
    Pythagoras's youth on, 14
Semicircle, 31, 33
    students of, 31, 33
solar eclipse, 17
soul
    Egyptian concept of, 26
    Pherecydes's teachings on, 13
    Pythagorean ideas about, 40, 43–44, 49, 52–53, 59, 64, 78, 92
square numbers, 67, 71–73
students, in Pythagorean society on Croton, 38–44, 46, 47
    daily routine of, 47

diet of, 44, 46
failure of, 43
screening process for, 42
vow of silence of, 42

T

Thales, 14–15, 16, 17, 19–20, 69
Theano (wife of Pythagoras), 46, 48
transmigration of the soul, 13, 52, 92
triangular numbers, 66, 71

U

universe, 14, 16, 49–50, 64, 73, 75–76, 90, 92–93
    infinite, 17, 19, 80

W

wine, 19, 20, 31, 56, 58
    Pythagorean restrictions on, 46

Z

Zeus, 75

ABOUT THE AUTHORS

Louis C. Coakley has been fascinated with the ancient world since childhood. He was intrigued by the way in which various ancient cultures—the Egyptians, Phoenicians, Babylonians, Persians, and Greeks—mix in the story of Pythagoras. A native of Massachusetts, he now lives in New Jersey.

Dimitra Karamanides earned her master's degree in European history and has been an ancient Greek history and philosophy enthusiast since her early teens. She has lived, worked, and traveled extensively in Greece, including visits to relatives in Miletus— the hometown of Thales, Pythagoras's teacher and mentor, and the birthplace of materialism and modern scientific thought. She has also visited several of the ancient oracles, including at Delphi and Dodoni. Today, she lives outside Philadelphia, Pennsylvania, with her husband, Chris, and two sons, Alexandros and Petros.

PHOTO CREDITS